Chocolate, A Glacier Grizzly

Written by: Peggy Christian

Illustrated by: Carol Cottone-Kolthoff

Dedicated to the rangers, researchers and citizens who work tirelessly for the protection of the grizzly bear and it's habitat
~ Peggy Christian

For Dave and Katie Kolthoff with love...
Thanks for your constant support,
encouragement and laughter!
~ Carol Cottone-Kolthoff

The Benefactory

HSUS
The Humane
Society of the
United States

There is a place so wild, that wolves and eagles, mountain lions and grizzly bears still roam free. Once these animals lived all over the western United States.

But people came, looking for new places to make their homes. They built roads and cities. They mined and logged and farmed the land. The wild animals might have disappeared. But in the early 1900's National Parks were created to save the last bits of wilderness and the animals that call it home.

This is the story of one of those parks, Glacier, in the northern Rocky Mountains. And it is the story of one of those animals, a grizzly bear cub, born there one winter in a dark, cozy den.

The cub weighed less than a pound and was smaller than one of her mother's paws. She had a blonde back and chocolate-colored legs. All winter, Chocolate drank her mother's rich milk and grew bigger and stronger.

By springtime, the den was getting crowded. One day, Chocolate's mother dug away the snow that still covered the entrance. The little cub blinked in the bright sunlight. It hurt her eyes at first. But exciting new smells reached her nose and Chocolate was curious.

Chocolate's mother was still sleepy after hibernating six months. But Chocolate wanted to look around. She turned over rocks and tossed sticks up with her nose. She ran up the snowy slope. She lost her footing and slid back down on her bottom. It was fun. She climbed back up and did it again.

Chocolate's mother soon headed down the mountain looking for food. They reached the forest and Chocolate's mother lifted her head at the sound of squawking ravens. She swung her head from side to side, wrinkling her nose. A heavy smell came from the trees. Chocolate followed her mother to the carcass of a winter-killed elk. Chocolate's mother eagerly bit into the meat.

Suddenly they heard a loud "whompf." A large male grizzly charged toward them. Chocolate hid behind her mother. Her mother roared and grunted, "Rooorr-huff-huff-huff." The male was after her cub. Bravely she charged. They came together, their heads twisting and turning. Chocolate's mother jumped back and the male rose up on his hind legs. Then he caught the scent of the elk and turned his head. Chocolate's mother raced back to Chocolate. They galloped off as the male grizzly settled down to feed on the carcass.

$\mathcal{A}$fter that Chocolate knew her place was close by her mother's side. Chocolate nursed, and grew fast. But Chocolate's mother needed to eat all the time, to build the fat she would need over the winter.

One day Chocolate's mother stopped in a field of flowers. She reached out with her front paw and raked the dirt with her long claws. What was her mother doing? Chocolate watched as her mother ate something from the ground.

Chocolate dug with her own sharp claws and then bit the dirt. She spat it out. It was awful. Chocolate's mother huffed at her and Chocolate saw her lift something white in her teeth. Chocolate snatched it from her. The alpine bistort bulb was sweet and juicy. Chocolate eagerly dug for more.

All summer they wandered, covering about a hundred square miles as they looked for food. Nighttime came earlier and earlier each day. Storms blowing out of the north brought snow mixed with rain. It was time for the bears to hibernate. High on a north-facing mountain side, Chocolate's mother searched for a place to den.

She stopped and stuck her nose between a mass of tree roots. She grunted with satisfaction. Rocks and dirt flew down the slope as Chocolate and her mother began digging. Working together, they dragged in mosses and grasses to line their cozy hole. Then they snuggled down inside.

11

$\mathcal{B}$y Chocolate's third summer, her mother's milk was drying up. It was time for Chocolate to go off on her own. Her mother began pushing Chocolate away, swatting at her or biting her neck. Then one evening as Chocolate and her mother were tearing rotten logs apart, looking for grubs, a big male grizzly crashed through the brush toward them. He leaped towards Chocolate. His front paw swung at her as she turned to run. She felt the sting of his claws in her hip. Hiding behind a rock, Chocolate waited for her mother to fight the bear off.

But her mother did not growl or charge the big male. She lowered her head and grunted softly. They touched noses. Then, huffing and puffing quietly, they circled each other. Chocolate's mother spun around and trotted over the hill. The male followed close behind.

$\mathcal{N}$ow Chocolate was all alone. Her hip still stinging, she wandered until she came to a cool stream. She soaked her hip and then saw a tall spruce where she could scratch her back. But the bark had deep long grooves and bits of bear hair. Another bear had marked this territory. Chocolate kept moving.

Chocolate's search pushed her farther and farther from the valley where she'd grown up. Several times she was chased away by other bears. Finally, she wandered into the Many Glacier Valley.

To Chocolate, it seemed she had found her place at last. No other grizzlies came to chase her away. She found plenty of food.

One morning, as she was stripping the juicy huckleberries from a branch, she smelled something odd. Peering through the bushes, she saw a strange creature. It was smaller than a bear, but stood on two hind legs.

Chocolate was not going to be chased away from her new-found home. She grunted and stepped toward the creature. It made a frightened noise and slowly backed away. Satisfied, Chocolate watched it disappear, then went back to sniffing out the sweet huckleberries.

The next day, Chocolate wandered down to the edge of
a large lake for a drink. Her nose picked up the smell of
another two-legged creature. To get a better look, she rose
on her hind legs. This time there were three of them.

"Look, a grizzly," said a man. "Be calm, and back away
slowly." The creatures moved toward a small stand of
aspen trees. Chocolate dropped back down on her front
paws. The creatures were no threat at all.

*P*ark rangers in Many Glacier began to get reports from hikers and tourists about a chocolate-legged grizzly bear. "This is no place for a grizzly. It will get in trouble, so close to trails and campgrounds," a ranger said.

"But the bear hasn't attacked anyone," said another.

"No, but she isn't afraid of them either," replied the ranger. "It's only a matter of time until the bear finds food in some-one's backpack, or in the garbage. Once the bear connects food and people, she'll be dangerous. We'll have to find a way to move her back into the wilderness."

In late July, three rangers tracked Chocolate as she nibbled on horsetails. Chocolate heard a rustling in the bushes and saw a flash of light. She felt a pinch in her shoulder as the ranger's dart stuck there.

Chocolate felt dizzy. She staggered away. The rangers followed. Again, Chocolate felt a pinch in her side. Feeling very sleepy, she looked for a soft place to bed down. Soon Chocolate was asleep.

The rangers measured Chocolate and checked her teeth to see how old she was. "She's a little thin, but healthy," said the ranger as he put a tag in her ear, so they could identify her later.

He slipped a radio collar around her neck. "Now we can use the signal to follow her and make sure she stays out of trouble." The collar had a strip made of cloth that would rot away in three years, letting the radio collar drop off.

They loaded the still sleeping Chocolate into a big sling hanging from a helicopter. Even the loud "thwack, thwack" of the helicopter blades overhead did not wake Chocolate up.

The rangers flew her out of the Many Glacier Valley. They flew her over mountains and rivers, across fields and valleys, until they were deep in the heart of Glacier Park. Then they carefully lowered her to the ground.

"Fold her legs under her so it will be easier for her to breathe." The ranger gave her a shot to wake her up, and they all moved a safe distance away.

Chocolate opened her eyes, feeling like she'd been in the deep sleep of hibernation. She got to her legs unsteadily. She felt something around her neck and tried to scratch it off, but it stuck there.

Lifting her nose high in the air, she took a deep sniff. The sweet scent of thimbleberries reached her nostrils and she walked off in search of them.

"Good work. Let's hope she stays in her new home," said one of the rangers.

25

A few days later, Chocolate was fishing in a stream when she heard twigs breaking. She turned and saw a big female grizzly and her yearling cub. Chocolate was frightened and backed off, waiting for the mother bear to attack. The female ruffled up her neck fur and paced back and forth. For several minutes the two bears stared at each other.

Then the big female started slowly toward Chocolate. Chocolate put her head down to show she was no threat. The big grizzly sniffed Chocolate's neck and back. Then she snorted to her cub and they joined Chocolate fishing in the stream. Chocolate gratefully stayed with the mother bear and her cub until she had learned her way around her new home.

$\mathcal{L}$ate that fall, as Chocolate was digging for roots through the first snowfall, she heard a loud buzzing overhead. She looked up and saw some kind of large white bird. She went back to her digging.

In the plane above her, the rangers were looking for Chocolate. The signal from her radio collar beeped loudly. "There she is," shouted one of the rangers, looking through her binoculars. "She's staying close to where we dropped her off."

Every few months the rangers tracked Chocolate with the radio collar. They followed her as she traveled through valleys and up ridges in search of food. "This bear is safe now. It looks like she'll stay in her new home and away from people," the ranger said.

Two years later, as Chocolate emerged from her den, something dropped from her neck. She nosed it, but she was eager to get to the valley and the first sweet grasses of spring.

A month later, the rangers found Chocolate's radio collar near the rock cave where she had denned. It had fallen off, just as it was supposed to.

The next fall, as Chocolate was getting up from her daybed, she caught the whiff of another bear. She saw a huge male grizzly lurking nearby in the woods. She turned to run, but the male did not charge her. He was not trying to scare her away. He was looking for a mate.

That winter, in a dark, cozy den high on a mountainside in Glacier Park, Chocolate gave birth to her first cub. The cub would nurse and grow until spring. Then Chocolate would begin teaching her cub about living in that wild place, where wolves and eagles, mountain lions and one special grizzly bear still roam free.

Glossary

Roam	wander
Created	made
Wilderness	wild, natural area
Den	cave where a wild animal sleeps
Entrance	the way in
Curious	interested
Hibernating	sleeping all winter
Carcass	body
Scent	smell
Galloped	ran fast
Nursed	drank mother's milk
Snatched	grabbed
Alpine bistort bulb	the bulb of a mountain plant
Swatting	hitting
Spun	turned in a circle
Huckleberries	a small wild fruit
Peering	looking
Creature	a living animal
Threat	danger
Attacked	to fall upon with force
Dangerous	harmful
Horsetails	a flowerless plant like a fern
Rustling	many small sounds in a row
Dart	a short, sharp arrow
Thimbleberries	a small wild fruit
Yearling	an animal that is a year old
Emerged	came out of
Eager	excited, very interested

the real Chocolate

Special thanks to Kate Kendall, at Glacier National Park, for all her help in providing research, photographs and other information regarding Chocolate's story.

The Humane Society of the United States, a non-profit organization founded in 1954, and with a constituency of over 4 million persons, is dedicated to speaking for animals, who cannot speak for themselves. The HSUS is devoted to making the world safe for animals through legal, educational, legislative and investigative means. The HSUS believes that humans have a moral obligation to protect other species with which we share the Earth. Co-sponsorship of this book by The Humane Society of the United States does not imply any partnership, joint venture, or other direct affiliation between The HSUS and Glacier National Park. For information on The HSUS, call: (202) 452-1100.

Printed by Horowitz/Rae Book Manufacturers, Inc.

Designed by Anita Soos Design, Inc.

Color Separations by Viking Color Separations Inc.

The Benefactory
One Post Road
Fairfield, CT 06430

Published by The Benefactory, Inc.
One Post Road, Fairfield, CT 06430
The Benefactory produces books, tapes and toys that foster animal protection and environmental preservation.
Call: (203) 255-7744

ISBN 1-882728-66-1
Printed in the U.S.A.
10 9 8 7 6 5 4 3 2 1